Table of Contents

1.

2.

3.

4.

    a.

b.

c.

d.

e.

f.

g.

h.

i.

j.

k.

l.

m.

n.

o.

p.

q.

r.

s.

t.

u.

The Magic of Chat GPT: How OpenAI is Advancing Natural Language Generation

Marc Ferrari

The Magic of Chat GPT: How OpenAI is Advancing Natural Language GenerationCopyright © 2023 by Marc Ferrari
All rights reserved.

*"I think Artificial Intelligence is probably
the single biggest item in the near term
that's likely to affect humanity."*

Elon Musk
Founder, CEO and chief engineer of Space X,
CEO and product architect of Tesla,
owner and CEO of Twitter,
founder of The Boring Company,
co-founder of Neuralink and OpenAI

The Magic of Chat GPT: How OpenAI is Advancing Natural Language Generation

Introduction to Chat GPT
and OpenAI's Language Models

An overview of the technology and its creators

Hey there! Are you interested in learning more about Chat GPT and how it's revolutionizing natural language processing? If so, you've come to the right place! In this chapter, we'll explore the ins and outs of this cutting-edge technology, and take a closer look at its creators, OpenAI.

So, what is Chat GPT? At its core, it's a deep learning model that can generate human-like text, making it a powerful tool for language generation, machine translation, and chatbot development. The technology is based on the transformer architecture, which is a type of neural network that excels at processing sequential data like language. Chat GPT models are pre-trained on massive datasets of text to learn the underlying patterns and structures of language, and can then be fine-tuned for specific tasks.

Now, let's talk about the people behind the technology. OpenAI was founded in 2015 by a group of tech luminaries, including Elon Musk, Sam Altman, Greg Brockman, Ilya Sutskever, John Schulman, and Wojciech Zaremba. The organization's mission is to develop advanced AI in a way that is safe and beneficial for humanity. They believe that AI has the potential to revolutionize the world, but that it must be developed in a responsible and ethical way.

One of the biggest challenges in AI research is developing machines that can understand and generate human language. Language is complex, nuanced, and often ambiguous, making it a difficult task for machines to replicate. However, with the development of deep learning models like Chat GPT, AI researchers have made significant strides in this area.

OpenAI has released several versions of the Chat GPT model, each one more advanced than the last. The original Chat GPT model was released in June 2018, followed by Chat GPT-2 in February 2019, and Chat GPT-3 in June 2020. Chat GPT-3 is currently the most advanced version of the model, with 175 billion parameters and the ability to generate a wide range of text with impressive accuracy and coherence.

One of the unique features of Chat GPT is its ability to generate text that is highly convincing and difficult to distinguish from human writing. This has raised concerns about the potential misuse of the technology, such as the creation of fake news or other forms of disinformation. To address these concerns, OpenAI has taken a responsible approach to the release of Chat GPT, limiting access to the model and carefully monitoring its use.

Chat GPT is a powerful technology that has the potential to revolutionize the field of natural language processing. Its ability to generate human-like text is impressive and holds promise for a wide range of applications. With the ongoing development of this technology, we can expect to see even more advanced AI language models in the near future. And the best part? OpenAI is dedicated to developing this technology in a responsible and ethical way, ensuring that it benefits humanity in the long run.

The Creation of OpenAI:
A Brief History and Purpose

OpenAI is an artificial intelligence research organization founded in December 2015 by a group of prominent tech entrepreneurs, including Elon Musk, Sam Altman, Greg Brockman, Ilya Sutskever, John Schulman, and Wojciech Zaremba. The goal of the organization is to promote and develop artificial intelligence in a safe and beneficial way for society.

The idea for OpenAI came about when Musk and Altman were discussing the potential risks of artificial intelligence. They believed that it was important to create a platform for developing AI that would prioritize safety, transparency, and collaboration. The organization was founded with a commitment to open research and a focus on developing AI for the betterment of humanity.

The initial funding for OpenAI came from its founders, who invested $1 billion to establish the organization as a non-profit entity. OpenAI's structure as a non-profit organization was a deliberate choice, as it allows the group to focus on its mission of advancing AI research and ensuring that the benefits of AI are widely shared. By operating as a non-profit, OpenAI can pursue its research goals without being constrained by profit motives.

OpenAI's research focuses on a range of topics, including natural language processing, robotics, and computer vision. The organization has made significant contributions to the field of AI, including the development of the GPT

(Generative Pre-trained Transformer) language model, which has revolutionized natural language processing.

OpenAI has also contributed to a number of real-world applications, such as improving healthcare through AI-assisted diagnosis and treatment, developing AI systems for autonomous vehicles, and enhancing cybersecurity through advanced threat detection.

In addition to its research efforts, OpenAI is committed to promoting the ethical and responsible use of AI. The organization advocates for transparency and accountability in AI development, and works to ensure that the benefits of AI are widely distributed.

OpenAI has become a leader in the field of AI research, and has attracted top talent from around the world. Its research has been published in top academic journals and presented at leading conferences, and the organization has collaborated with a range of partners, including governments, academic institutions, and businesses.

While OpenAI is still relatively young, its impact on the field of AI has been significant. The organization has helped to advance the development of safe and beneficial AI, and has positioned itself as a leader in promoting ethical AI practices. With its commitment to open research and collaboration, OpenAI is well positioned to continue making important contributions to the field of AI and the betterment of society as a whole.

Natural Language Processing:
A Brief History

A look at the evolution of NLP and how Chat GPT fits in

Welcome to a brief journey through the history of Natural Language Processing (NLP), a fascinating field of computer science that deals with the interaction between computers and human language. In this chapter, we'll explore the evolution of NLP, from its early beginnings to the present day, and how Chat GPT fits into this picture.

Early History

The early days of NLP date back to the 1950s, when researchers started exploring the possibility of machine translation. At first, they focused on creating rules-based systems that could translate words and phrases from one language to another. However, these systems were limited by their rigidity and inability to account for the nuances of human language. This prompted researchers to seek more flexible and adaptable solutions.

In the 1960s and 1970s, statistical models for language processing began to emerge. These models were based on probabilistic algorithms that could learn from large amounts of data, making them more flexible and adaptable than their rules-based counterparts. However, the limitations of computing power at the time made it difficult to apply these models to real-world problems.

Recent Advancements

In recent years, NLP has made significant strides, thanks in large part to the development of deep learning models like Chat GPT. These models are based on artificial neural networks that can learn from vast amounts of data to recognize patterns and make predictions. This has revolutionized the field of NLP, enabling machines to understand and generate language with increasing accuracy and fluency.

Chat GPT is a prime example of how deep learning models have transformed NLP. The model is pre-trained on massive datasets of text, enabling it to learn the underlying patterns and structures of language. This allows it to generate text that is highly convincing and difficult to distinguish from human writing.

Applications of NLP

NLP has a wide range of applications across various industries. One of the most common applications is in the development of chatbots and virtual assistants. These tools use NLP algorithms to understand user queries and generate responses in a natural and intuitive way.

NLP is also used in sentiment analysis, which involves analyzing large amounts of text data to determine the overall sentiment of a given piece of content. This can be used to track consumer sentiment towards a particular brand or product, for example.

Another application of NLP is in machine translation, which involves automatically translating text from one language to another. While early efforts in machine translation were limited by their rules-based approach, deep learning models like Chat GPT have made significant strides in this area, enabling more accurate and natural translations.

NLP has come a long way since its early days of rules-based systems and statistical models. The development of deep learning models like Chat GPT has revolutionized the field, enabling machines to understand and generate natural language with increasing accuracy and fluency. As the technology continues to evolve, we can expect to see even more exciting applications of NLP in the years to come.

Understanding Chat GPT's Architecture

A deep dive into how the system works

Chat GPT is a fascinating technology that is taking the world of natural language processing by storm. This chapter will delve deeper into the architecture of Chat GPT, exploring how the system works and why it is so effective at generating natural language.

Transformer-Based Architecture

At the heart of Chat GPT is a transformer-based architecture that utilizes multiple layers of artificial neural networks. These networks are trained on vast amounts of text data, enabling the model to learn the complex structures and patterns of language.

The transformer-based architecture is particularly powerful because it enables the model to process entire sequences of text, as opposed to just individual words or phrases. This allows the model to capture the context and meaning of the text, making it better at generating natural and convincing language.

Pre-Training and Fine-Tuning

Before it can be used for specific tasks, Chat GPT must first undergo a pre-training process. During pre-training, the model is exposed to vast amounts of text data, such as Wikipedia and the Common Crawl. This unsupervised learning approach allows the model to learn on its own, discovering the underlying structures and patterns of language.

Once pre-training is complete, the model can be fine-tuned for specific tasks, such as language translation or text generation. Fine-tuning involves training the model on smaller datasets of text that are specific to the task at hand, allowing it to specialize in that area.

The fine-tuning process typically involves using a smaller learning rate and a smaller batch size than the pre-training process. This helps prevent overfitting, improving the model's ability to generalize to new data.

Generation Process

When generating text, Chat GPT takes a seed text as input and uses its trained neural networks to generate a continuation of the text. The model generates text one token at a time, with each token being generated based on the probability distribution of possible tokens given the preceding text.

The generation process can be controlled by adjusting various parameters, such as the length of the generated text, the temperature of the probability distribution, and the presence of specific keywords or phrases.

One of the most impressive features of Chat GPT is its ability to generate highly coherent and natural-sounding text. This is accomplished by incorporating context into the generation process, allowing the model to generate text that fits seamlessly into the surrounding content.

Applications of Chat GPT

Chat GPT has a wide range of applications in various industries. One of the most common applications is in the development of chatbots and virtual assistants, which can use the model to generate natural and convincing responses to user queries.

The model can also be used for text completion and language translation, among other tasks. As the technology continues to improve, we can expect to see even more exciting applications of Chat GPT in the years to come.

The architecture of Chat GPT is based on a powerful transformer-based model that can process entire sequences of text, allowing it to capture the context and meaning of the text. The model is pre-trained on massive datasets of text and can be fine-tuned for specific tasks. When generating text, Chat GPT uses a probability distribution to generate each token, resulting in highly coherent and natural-sounding text. With its wide range of applications and impressive performance, Chat GPT is sure to continue to be a key player in the field of natural language generation.

Training Chat GPT:
The Process Behind the Magic

An explanation of how the AI model is trained

Training Chat GPT is a fascinating and intricate process that involves collecting vast amounts of data, preprocessing it, designing the model architecture, and fine-tuning the model for specific tasks. In this chapter, we'll delve deeper into each of these stages to provide a more detailed understanding of how Chat GPT is trained.

Data Collection

Data collection is the first and most crucial step in training Chat GPT. The model requires a large corpus of text data to learn from, and this data must be diverse, representative of the language it will generate, and free from errors or inconsistencies.

The data can come from various sources, such as books, news articles, and online forums. However, it's essential to ensure that the data is carefully selected to avoid bias and to represent the language that the model will generate accurately.

Preprocessing

After collecting the data, it must be preprocessed to prepare it for training. Preprocessing involves cleaning the data and breaking it down into smaller units called tokens.

Each token is assigned a unique identifier or numerical value, which the model uses to learn from the data.

Preprocessing also involves removing stop words and other noise from the data, such as punctuation and special characters. This helps to reduce the complexity of the data and allows the model to focus on the most important aspects of the language.

Model Architecture

The model architecture is the next critical aspect of training Chat GPT. The architecture is designed to take in a sequence of tokens as input and generate a sequence of tokens as output. This is achieved using a transformer-based architecture that comprises multiple layers of artificial neural networks.

Each layer in the model is responsible for processing the input and generating a prediction for the next token in the sequence. During training, the weights of the neural network are adjusted to minimize the difference between the predicted output and the actual output.

Training

The training process involves feeding the model sequences of tokens as input and the corresponding sequences of tokens as output. The model then generates a prediction for the next token in the sequence, and the difference between the prediction and the actual output is calculated using a loss function.

The weights of the neural network are then adjusted to minimize the loss function, improving the model's ability to predict the correct output. This process is repeated multiple times, with the model's performance improving with each iteration.

Fine-Tuning

Once the model has been trained on a large dataset of text, it can be fine-tuned for specific tasks. Fine-tuning involves training the model on a smaller dataset of text that is specific to the task at hand.

For example, if the model is being fine-tuned for language translation, it will be trained on a smaller dataset of text that includes translations from one language to another. This allows the model to specialize in the specific task and improve its performance.

Training Chat GPT is a complex and challenging process that requires careful consideration at each stage. From collecting and preprocessing data to designing the model architecture and fine-tuning the model, each step plays a critical role in the model's ability to generate natural-sounding language.

As the field of AI and natural language processing continues to advance, we can expect to see even more impressive language generation technologies in the years to come. By understanding the process behind training

Chat GPT, we can appreciate the level of sophistication and expertise required to create such groundbreaking technology.

The Importance of Large Datasets in Natural Language Generation

How the quality and size of the data affects Chat GPT's output

Natural language generation (NLG) is a rapidly growing field that involves creating software that can generate natural-sounding language from data. To achieve this, NLG systems like Chat GPT require a large dataset to learn from, which can significantly affect their output.

The importance of large datasets in natural language generation stems from the fact that they allow the model to learn from a vast amount of diverse language data. This exposure to diverse language and contexts is essential for the model to produce natural-sounding language that is representative of the language it is designed to mimic. With more data, the model can recognize and learn from patterns and relationships within the data, allowing it to generate more accurate language.

However, the size of the dataset alone is not enough. The quality of the data is equally important as it can impact the output of the model. Noisy, inconsistent, or biased data can introduce errors into the model, leading to unnatural-sounding language. Therefore, it's essential to ensure that the data used to train the model is of high quality and representative of the language it will generate. This requires careful curation and preprocessing of the data to remove any noise, errors, or inconsistencies.

The future of large datasets in natural language generation is promising, with increasing availability of digital text data. With more data, it will be possible to create even more sophisticated NLG models that can be used for a wider range of applications. In addition to larger datasets, specialized datasets designed for specific tasks, such as sentiment analysis or language translation, can also enable the creation of more specialized models.

The quality and size of the dataset used to train NLG models like Chat GPT are crucial to their performance. Large datasets allow for exposure to diverse language and contexts, while high-quality data ensures that the model produces natural-sounding language. With the continued development of NLG technologies, the importance of large datasets will only increase, leading to more advanced and specialized NLG models that can be used for a variety of applications.

Fine-Tuning Chat GPT for Specific Applications

How businesses and organizations can customize the AI model for their needs

Fine-tuning Chat GPT for specific applications has become a popular practice for businesses and organizations looking to improve the accuracy and effectiveness of their language generation. By creating language models that are tailored to their specific needs, businesses and organizations can save time and resources while having greater control over the language generated.

One of the primary benefits of fine-tuning Chat GPT is the ability to create more accurate and natural-sounding language. Pre-trained language models like Chat GPT are trained on large, diverse datasets that provide a general understanding of language and context. However, these models may not always produce language that is specific to a particular domain or task. By fine-tuning the model on a dataset specific to the domain or task, the model can learn the nuances of the language and produce more accurate and effective language.

Another benefit of fine-tuning Chat GPT is the ability to save time and resources. Creating a language model from scratch requires a large dataset and significant computing resources. Fine-tuning a pre-trained model like Chat GPT on a smaller dataset specific to the domain or task can result in a language model that is just as accurate but requires less time and resources to create.

Lastly, fine-tuning Chat GPT allows businesses and organizations to have greater control over the language generated by the model. By fine-tuning the model, businesses and organizations can ensure that the language generated by the model is consistent with their brand voice and tone. This level of control is especially important for businesses and organizations with strict guidelines for language use and consistency.

The process of fine-tuning Chat GPT for specific applications involves several steps. Firstly, businesses and organizations must identify the domain or task that the model will be used for. This step is crucial as it determines the dataset that will be used for fine-tuning. Once the domain or task is identified, businesses and organizations must gather a dataset specific to the domain or task. This dataset should be representative of the language and context of the domain and of high quality.

After obtaining the dataset, the model is fine-tuned using transfer learning techniques. Transfer learning involves taking the pre-trained model and adapting it to the specific domain or task by fine-tuning the weights of the model's layers to better fit the new data. This process allows the model to retain its general language generation capabilities while adapting to the nuances of the specific task or domain.

Fine-tuning Chat GPT for specific applications is an effective way for businesses and organizations to create language models that are tailored to their specific needs. The benefits of fine-tuning Chat GPT include more accurate and natural-sounding language, saving time and resources, and greater control over the language generated by the model. The process of fine-tuning involves identifying the domain or task, gathering a high-quality dataset, and fine-tuning the model using transfer learning techniques. By fine-tuning Chat GPT, businesses and organizations can improve the accuracy and effectiveness of their language generation while saving time and resources.

The Role of Transformers
in Natural Language Processing

A discussion of the transformer architecture that powers Chat GPT

Transformers have brought about a major shift in the field of natural language processing (NLP), and have become a crucial component of OpenAI's Chat GPT. In this chapter, we will delve deeper into the inner workings of transformers and explore how they have transformed the landscape of NLP.

Traditional NLP models relied on recurrent neural networks (RNNs) to process sequential data like text. However, RNNs were not well-suited for processing long sequences of text and were computationally expensive. This limitation led to the development of transformers, which have become the go-to architecture for processing long sequences of text.

Transformers are a type of neural network architecture that processes input data in parallel, making them more efficient and effective for processing long sequences of text. The architecture of transformers consists of an encoder and decoder, with the encoder converting the input sequence of text into a series of vectors, and the decoder generating the output sequence of text based on those vectors.

The key innovation of transformers is the self-attention mechanism. This mechanism enables the model to focus on different parts of the input sequence when generating the output sequence. Self-attention is achieved through multi-head attention, where the input sequence is processed by multiple attention heads in parallel. Each attention head learns to attend to different parts of the input sequence, allowing the model to capture complex relationships between different parts of the sequence.

Positional encoding is another critical component of transformers. Since transformers process input sequences in parallel, they do not inherently have information about the order of the sequence. Positional encoding provides this information by adding a fixed-length vector to each input token that encodes its position in the sequence. This ensures that the model can capture the sequential relationships between tokens.

Transformers have enabled the development of large-scale language models like Chat GPT, which can generate natural-sounding text. Chat GPT is particularly impressive because it can generate text that is coherent and contextually relevant, even when given only a few words of input. The ability to generate high-quality text has significant implications for various industries, including customer service, content creation, and language translation.

Transformers have revolutionized the field of NLP and have played a crucial role in the development of language models like Chat GPT. The self-attention mechanism and positional encoding have enabled transformers to process long sequences of text efficiently and effectively, leading to the development of language models that can generate natural-sounding text. As NLP continues to evolve, it is likely that transformers will continue to be at the forefront of this exciting field.

Exploring the Limitations of Chat GPT

An examination of the challenges the system still faces

Chat GPT has undoubtedly made incredible strides in the field of natural language processing. However, as with any technology, it is important to recognize that there are still limitations and challenges that need to be addressed. In this chapter, we will explore some of the limitations of Chat GPT in more detail.

One of the most significant limitations of Chat GPT is its lack of real-world knowledge. While the system can generate coherent and contextually relevant text, it does not have a deep understanding of the world. This means that it can struggle with tasks that require background knowledge or common sense reasoning. For example, if asked a question like "Why do humans need oxygen to breathe?", Chat GPT may struggle to provide a detailed answer, despite its ability to generate fluent text. This is because the system lacks the real-world knowledge necessary to fully understand the question and provide an accurate answer.

Another limitation of Chat GPT is its susceptibility to biases in the training data. Like all language models, Chat GPT relies heavily on the quality and quantity of the data it is trained on. If the training data contains biases or inaccuracies, the model is likely to reproduce these biases in its output. This can have serious implications for applications like automated content moderation, where the system's biases can perpetuate harmful stereotypes and misinformation. Addressing this limitation requires careful curation of the training data and ongoing monitoring of the system's output to ensure that it is not reproducing harmful biases.

Chat GPT also struggles with understanding context beyond the immediate context of the input. While it can generate text that is relevant to the input text, it may not be able to incorporate information from previous or subsequent interactions. This limitation can lead to issues like repetitive responses or inconsistencies in the system's output. This is particularly challenging for conversational AI applications, where the ability to maintain a coherent and engaging conversation is critical.

Finally, Chat GPT is still limited by the computational resources required to train and run the model. While the system is incredibly powerful, it still requires significant amounts of computing power and storage capacity. This can make it challenging for individuals or small organizations to use the system effectively. As the field of natural language processing continues to evolve, however, it is likely that this limitation will be addressed through advances in hardware and software optimization.

While Chat GPT is a remarkable achievement in the field of natural language processing, it is important to recognize that there are still limitations and challenges that need to be addressed. By understanding these limitations and working to address them, we can continue to improve the capabilities of Chat GPT and other natural language processing   technologies.

Chat GPT and
the Future of Chatbots

How the technology is advancing the chatbot industry

The emergence of chatbots in recent years has revolutionized the way businesses and organizations interact with customers. Chatbots offer a convenient and efficient way to provide support, answer inquiries, and engage with customers in real-time. However, traditional chatbots have often been limited in their ability to understand and generate natural language, resulting in stilted and awkward interactions.

Enter Chat GPT, the AI model developed by OpenAI. Chat GPT uses advanced natural language processing (NLP) techniques to generate contextually relevant and fluent text, enabling more natural and engaging conversations with customers. With its ability to generate high-quality text, Chat GPT has quickly become one of the most exciting advancements in the field of conversational AI.

One of the key benefits of Chat GPT is its flexibility. The system can be fine-tuned and customized for specific applications, allowing businesses to tailor the AI model to their needs. This means that chatbots powered by Chat GPT can be used across a range of industries and use cases, from customer support to sales and marketing. By integrating Chat GPT into chatbot platforms, businesses can provide a more human-like experience for customers, leading to increased customer satisfaction and loyalty.

Another significant advantage of Chat GPT is its ability to generate text in multiple languages. This feature makes it an ideal solution for businesses that operate globally and need to communicate with customers in different regions and countries. Chatbots powered by Chat GPT can provide multilingual support and assistance, improving the accessibility of businesses to customers worldwide.

Looking ahead, the future of chatbots powered by Chat GPT looks very promising. As the technology continues to evolve and improve, we can expect to see even more advanced chatbots that are capable of engaging in deeper and more complex conversations. These chatbots will be able to handle more sophisticated inquiries and provide even more personalized support to customers, improving the customer experience and driving business results.

Chat GPT represents a significant advancement in the field of conversational AI and has the potential to transform the chatbot industry. With its ability to generate high-quality text, flexibility, and multilingual support, Chat GPT is quickly becoming the preferred solution for businesses looking to provide more natural and engaging interactions with customers. As the technology continues to evolve, we can expect even more exciting developments in the field of conversational   AI.

Real-World Applications of Chat GPT

A showcase of how the technology is being used today

Chat GPT, the powerful natural language processing tool developed by OpenAI, has numerous real-world applications that are transforming various industries. In this chapter, we will explore some of the most notable applications of Chat GPT and how they are revolutionizing the way businesses and organizations operate.

Customer Service: Chat GPT has become an essential tool in the customer service industry, enabling companies to provide round-the-clock assistance to their customers. With the help of Chat GPT-powered chatbots, companies can handle a large volume of inquiries and resolve customer issues quickly and efficiently. The chatbots can understand natural language and provide personalized responses, making the customer experience seamless and hassle-free.

Content Creation: Content creation is another area where Chat GPT is making significant strides. With its ability to generate high-quality and unique content, Chat GPT is becoming a popular tool for content marketers and publishers. The system can generate product descriptions, social media posts, and even entire articles with little to no human input. This has the potential to transform the content creation industry, making it faster and more cost-effective.

Healthcare: Chat GPT is also being used in the healthcare industry to improve patient care. Chatbots powered by Chat GPT can assist patients with medication management, provide health advice, and even diagnose certain conditions. This has the potential to reduce the burden on healthcare professionals and improve patient outcomes.

Finance: The finance industry is also benefiting from Chat GPT's natural language processing capabilities. Chatbots powered by Chat GPT can assist customers with financial planning, investment advice, and even loan applications. This has the potential to streamline financial services and improve the customer experience.

Language Translation: Chat GPT is also being used to improve language translation services. The system can understand and translate multiple languages, making it a valuable tool for businesses operating in multiple countries. Chat GPT can provide accurate translations of product descriptions, marketing materials, and other content, enabling businesses to expand their reach and connect with new customers.

Education: Chat GPT can be used to develop intelligent tutoring systems that can assist students in their learning journey.

Sentiment Analysis: Chat GPT can be used to analyze the sentiment of social media posts, reviews, and customer feedback to understand public opinion and customer feedback.

Personalized Marketing: Chat GPT can be used to develop personalized marketing campaigns that can understand individual customer preferences and recommend products accordingly.

Virtual Assistants: Chat GPT can be used to power virtual assistants like Siri and Alexa that can help users perform tasks and answer queries.

Writing Assistance: Chat GPT can be used to provide writing assistance, including grammar and spell-check, and to generate ideas for content creation.

Legal Assistance: Chat GPT can be used to develop legal chatbots that can help people with legal queries and suggest legal documents.

Fraud Detection: Chat GPT can be used to detect fraudulent activities, including detecting fake reviews, spam messages, and online scams.

Gaming: Chat GPT can be used to create game characters that can interact with players and enhance their gaming experience.

Travel Assistance: Chat GPT can be used to develop travel chatbots that can help users with travel-related queries, including flight booking, hotel reservation, and destination suggestions.

News Aggregation: Chat GPT can be used to aggregate news from various sources and provide personalized news recommendations to users.

Mental Health: Chat GPT can be used to develop mental health chatbots that can help users deal with anxiety, depression, and other mental health issues.

Human Resources: Chat GPT can be used to develop HR chatbots that can assist employees with queries related to benefits, policies, and performance reviews.

Finance: Chat GPT can be used to develop finance chatbots that can assist users in managing their finances, including budgeting, savings, and investments.

Gaming Industry: Chat GPT can be used to develop chatbots for gaming companies to provide customers with support, suggestions, and product information.

Food and Beverages: Chat GPT can be used to develop chatbots for the food and beverages industry to take orders, provide recommendations, and answer customer queries.

Real Estate: Chat GPT can be used to develop chatbots for the real estate industry to provide customers with property recommendations, mortgage advice, and property valuation.

Chat GPT is a game-changing technology that is transforming various industries. Its natural language processing capabilities and ability to generate high-quality content make it a valuable tool for businesses and organizations of all kinds. As the technology continues to advance, we can expect to see even more innovative applications of Chat GPT in the years to come.

The Impact of Chat GPT
on Machine Translation

How the AI model is improving translation services

Machine translation, the process of automatically translating text from one language to another, has come a long way in recent years. And one of the driving forces behind this progress is the development of powerful natural language processing (NLP) tools like Chat GPT.

The traditional approach to machine translation relied on rules-based systems, where human linguists would create a set of rules for how one language should be translated into another. This approach, while effective in some cases, was limited by the fact that it required a great deal of human input and was unable to capture the nuances and complexities of natural language.

Chat GPT, on the other hand, uses a data-driven approach to translation. It has the ability to learn patterns and relationships between languages by analyzing large amounts of text data, and can then apply this knowledge to translate new text.

One of the key benefits of Chat GPT for machine translation is its ability to handle ambiguity and context. Because the system has been trained on a wide range of text data, it has the ability to recognize and account for different meanings of words based on their context. This means that it can produce more accurate translations, even when dealing with complex or ambiguous text.

Another advantage of Chat GPT for machine translation is its ability to adapt to new languages and domains. By fine-tuning the model on specific language pairs or domains, it is possible to create highly accurate and specialized translation systems.

One notable example of the use of Chat GPT in machine translation is Google's recently launched "Translatotron" system, which uses a modified version of the GPT-2 model to translate speech directly from one language to another. This system is able to produce translations that retain the speaker's voice and intonation, and has the potential to revolutionize the field of speech translation.

The impact of Chat GPT on machine translation is clear. By enabling more accurate and nuanced translations, and by opening up new possibilities for speech translation, the technology is helping to break down language barriers and bring people closer together.

Chat GPT's Contribution
to Voice Assistants

A discussion of how Chat GPT is being used in voice assistants like Alexa and Siri

Voice assistants like Amazon's Alexa and Apple's Siri have become an integral part of our daily lives. We use them to set reminders, play music, get directions, and even order groceries. These voice assistants use natural language processing technology to understand and respond to our commands, and Chat GPT has played a significant role in improving their capabilities.

One of the primary ways that Chat GPT has contributed to voice assistants is through its ability to generate more human-like responses. Voice assistants have traditionally used pre-programmed responses to answer user queries, but these responses can often sound robotic and lack the nuance and context that is present in human conversation. With Chat GPT, voice assistants can now generate responses that sound more natural and conversational, making the overall user experience much more pleasant.

Another way that Chat GPT has impacted voice assistants is through its ability to handle more complex queries. In the past, voice assistants were limited to responding to simple commands and questions, but with the help of Chat GPT, they can now understand and respond to more complex queries. For example, a user could ask, "What's the weather like in San Francisco next weekend?" and the voice assistant could provide a detailed response based on the user's location and the current weather conditions.

Chat GPT has also made it easier for voice assistants to understand different languages and accents. By training the AI model on large datasets of multilingual data, voice assistants can now recognize and respond to queries in multiple languages, making them more accessible to a global audience.

Chat GPT has had a significant impact on the capabilities of voice assistants, making them more human-like, better at handling complex queries, and more accessible to a global audience. As Chat GPT continues to evolve and improve, we can expect voice assistants to become even more advanced and useful in our daily lives.

The Ethics of Chat GPT: Implications for Society

A look at the social and ethical implications of the technology

As the capabilities of Chat GPT and other natural language generation models continue to grow, it is important to consider their social and ethical implications. The ability of these systems to generate human-like language opens up new possibilities for communication and automation, but also raises concerns about the potential misuse of the technology.

One of the primary ethical considerations when it comes to Chat GPT is the potential for the model to spread misinformation or generate harmful content. The technology is capable of generating text that is difficult to distinguish from human writing, which raises concerns about the spread of fake news or other types of harmful content. This is particularly concerning in the context of social media, where false information can spread rapidly and have real-world consequences.

Another ethical consideration is the potential for bias in the data used to train Chat GPT. Because the model is only as good as the data it is trained on, biases in the data can lead to biased or unfair outputs. For example, if the data used to train the model is biased against certain groups of people, the output generated by the model may also be biased.

Additionally, there is concern about the impact that Chat GPT and other natural language generation models may have on employment. As the technology continues to improve, it has the potential to automate many jobs that currently require human communication skills, such as customer service or content creation. This could lead to significant job displacement in certain industries.

It is important for developers and users of Chat GPT to consider these ethical implications and work to mitigate any potential negative impacts of the technology. This may include implementing measures to detect and filter out harmful content generated by the model, as well as taking steps to ensure that the data used to train the model is diverse and representative.

While Chat GPT and other natural language generation models have the potential to revolutionize communication and automation, it is important to approach their development and use with a critical eye towards their social and ethical implications.

Chat GPT's Role in Education

How the AI model is transforming the way we learn

As the field of artificial intelligence continues to evolve, it is increasingly becoming apparent that it has the potential to revolutionize various industries and sectors. Education is one such area where AI can have a significant impact. The ability of AI models like Chat GPT to understand and generate natural language makes them an attractive tool for educators looking to improve the learning experience.

The use of Chat GPT in education is still in its early stages, but the potential applications are numerous. One of the most exciting possibilities is the creation of intelligent tutoring systems that can provide personalized instruction to students based on their individual needs and learning styles. With its ability to generate human-like language, Chat GPT can help students better understand complex concepts and engage with the material in a more interactive and immersive way.

Another application of Chat GPT in education is in the creation of chatbots that can provide students with instant feedback and support. These chatbots can be programmed to answer questions, provide clarification on specific topics, and even offer suggestions on study strategies. With the growing demand for remote learning and online education, chatbots powered by Chat GPT can provide a more personalized and interactive learning experience for students who may not have access to a traditional classroom setting.

Furthermore, Chat GPT can be used to create language learning tools that enable students to practice their language skills in a realistic and engaging way. These tools can be programmed to respond to a wide range of inputs and provide instant feedback, allowing students to practice speaking and writing in a low-pressure environment.

However, like any other technology, there are ethical concerns associated with the use of Chat GPT in education. For example, there is a risk that the technology could be used to replace human educators entirely, leading to a loss of jobs and the devaluation of the teaching profession. It is important to ensure that the use of AI in education is not viewed as a replacement for human teachers, but rather as a supplement to their work.

Chat GPT has the potential to transform education by providing personalized, interactive, and engaging learning experiences to students. With its natural language processing capabilities, it can help educators create intelligent tutoring systems, chatbots, and language learning tools that are responsive to the needs and preferences of individual students. However, it is important to approach the use of AI in education with caution and ensure that its implementation is ethical and equitable.

Chat GPT and Journalism: Transforming News Writing

How Chat GPT is changing the way we consume and produce news

In recent years, there has been a surge of interest in how artificial intelligence (AI) can transform the way we consume and produce news. Chat GPT, with its advanced natural language generation capabilities, is at the forefront of this transformation. In this chapter, we will explore how Chat GPT is changing the landscape of journalism.

Traditional news writing involves a significant amount of manual labor. Journalists must conduct extensive research, analyze data, and distill complex information into clear and concise articles. However, with the help of AI, journalists can now automate many of these tasks, allowing them to focus on more creative and analytical aspects of news production.

One of the most significant ways Chat GPT is transforming journalism is through automated article generation. News organizations can now use Chat GPT to automatically generate articles on a wide range of topics. These articles can be customized to fit the tone and style of the publication, and can even include multimedia elements like images and videos.

In addition to automating article generation, Chat GPT can also be used to improve the speed and accuracy of fact-checking. By analyzing vast amounts of data, Chat GPT can quickly identify discrepancies and inconsistencies in reporting. This can help journalists ensure that their stories are accurate and reliable, reducing the risk of spreading misinformation.

Another way Chat GPT is transforming journalism is through personalized news delivery. By analyzing a user's browsing history and interests, Chat GPT can curate personalized news feeds that are tailored to their preferences. This not only enhances the user experience but also enables news organizations to better understand their audience and provide more relevant content.

However, as with any new technology, there are concerns about the potential impact of Chat GPT on the journalism industry. Some worry that the increasing use of automated article generation will lead to job losses and a reduction in the quality of journalism. Others are concerned about the potential for bias in AI-generated news articles.

To address these concerns, it is essential to ensure that Chat GPT is used ethically and responsibly. This means being transparent about how the technology is used, ensuring that it is not used to spread misinformation or propaganda, and ensuring that journalists and other media professionals are trained to use Chat GPT effectively.

Chat GPT is transforming the journalism industry by automating many of the manual tasks involved in news production, improving fact-checking, and enabling personalized news delivery. While there are concerns about the potential impact of AI on the industry, if used ethically and responsibly, Chat GPT has the potential to revolutionize the way we consume and produce news.

Using Chat GPT for Sentiment Analysis

How the technology is being used to gauge public opinion

Sentiment analysis is the process of identifying and extracting the emotions and opinions expressed in a piece of text. With the vast amount of text data available on the internet, sentiment analysis has become an essential tool for businesses and organizations to understand public opinion and make informed decisions. Chat GPT has emerged as a powerful tool for sentiment analysis, enabling businesses to process large amounts of text data and analyze sentiment on a massive scale.

Chat GPT's ability to understand natural language and generate text has made it an ideal tool for sentiment analysis. Its deep learning algorithms allow it to recognize patterns and trends in text data, and use them to accurately identify the emotions and opinions expressed. This has led to an increase in the accuracy and reliability of sentiment analysis, enabling businesses to make better decisions based on real-time feedback.

One of the key advantages of using Chat GPT for sentiment analysis is its ability to process large volumes of text data quickly and efficiently. This means that businesses can analyze large amounts of customer feedback, social media posts, and news articles in real-time, giving them a competitive advantage. Chat GPT's natural language processing capabilities also enable it to analyze text in multiple languages, making it an excellent tool for businesses with a global presence.

Another advantage of using Chat GPT for sentiment analysis is its ability to understand context. Unlike traditional sentiment analysis tools that rely on keyword analysis, Chat GPT can understand the meaning and context of text data, allowing it to provide more accurate sentiment analysis. For example, Chat GPT can recognize sarcasm and irony in text, allowing it to accurately identify negative sentiment even when it is expressed in a positive way.

Chat GPT's ability to analyze sentiment has many practical applications, including customer feedback analysis, reputation management, and brand monitoring. By analyzing customer feedback, businesses can gain insights into the strengths and weaknesses of their products and services, allowing them to make data-driven improvements. Reputation management and brand monitoring can also benefit from sentiment analysis, allowing businesses to identify and address negative sentiment before it affects their reputation.

Chat GPT's natural language processing capabilities and deep learning algorithms have made it a powerful tool for sentiment analysis. Its ability to process large volumes of text data quickly and accurately, while understanding context, has made it an essential tool for businesses and organizations looking to understand public opinion and make data-driven decisions. As the technology continues to evolve, we can expect to see Chat GPT being used in even more applications for sentiment analysis.

Chat GPT's Contribution to Content Creation

How the technology is being used to automate content creation

Chat GPT has been making waves in the field of natural language generation with its impressive ability to generate coherent and contextually relevant responses to text-based prompts. One area where this technology has shown particular promise is in content creation, where it is being used to automate the writing of news articles, product descriptions, and more.

The process of content creation can be time-consuming and labor-intensive, especially for large companies that need to produce a high volume of content on a regular basis. Chat GPT offers a solution to this problem by enabling businesses to automate the writing process, saving them both time and money.

One way Chat GPT is being used for content creation is through the generation of news articles. With the help of machine learning algorithms and large datasets, the AI model can analyze and summarize news stories from various sources, and then generate new articles based on this information. This can be especially useful for news outlets that need to cover a wide range of topics, but may not have the resources to do so manually.

Chat GPT is also being used to generate product descriptions for e-commerce websites. By analyzing the features and benefits of a product, the AI model can generate a compelling and informative description that is tailored to the target audience. This not only saves time for businesses, but can also help to improve the customer experience by providing accurate and detailed product information.

However, there are still some limitations to Chat GPT's ability to generate content. The AI model may struggle with more complex writing tasks, such as creative writing or technical writing, where there may be more nuances and specific rules to follow. Additionally, there is always the risk of producing content that is factually inaccurate or biased, which could have negative consequences for businesses and society as a whole.

Chat GPT's contribution to content creation is an exciting development that has the potential to transform the way we produce and consume content. As the technology continues to advance and improve, it will be interesting to see how businesses and industries continue to use it to their   advantage.

The Future of Chat GPT: Challenges and Opportunities

An analysis of where the technology is headed

Chat GPT and other natural language processing technologies have come a long way in a relatively short amount of time, and the future looks incredibly bright. However, there are still a number of challenges that must be addressed before the full potential of these tools can be realized.

One of the biggest challenges facing Chat GPT is the need for even larger and more diverse datasets. While the current models are capable of producing impressive results, they are limited by the quality and quantity of the data they have been trained on. In order to create more accurate and sophisticated AI models, researchers and developers must work to gather and organize vast amounts of text data from a wide range of sources.

Another challenge is the need for greater explainability in the output generated by these models. As AI becomes more prevalent in our lives, there is a growing demand for transparency and accountability. Many stakeholders, including business owners, policymakers, and the general public, want to understand how these models arrive at their conclusions and predictions.

However, there are also many exciting opportunities on the horizon for Chat GPT and other natural language processing tools. For example, these technologies have the potential to revolutionize education by creating personalized learning experiences for students. Chat GPT can also be used to automate a wide range of tasks, from customer service to content creation, freeing up valuable time and resources for businesses.

In addition, as AI continues to advance, we may see the development of even more sophisticated and nuanced natural language processing tools. These models could have a wide range of applications, from language translation to speech recognition to chatbot conversations.

The future of Chat GPT and natural language processing is full of both challenges and opportunities. While there is still much work to be done to improve the accuracy, explainability, and usability of these technologies, the potential benefits are enormous. As researchers and developers continue to push the boundaries of what is possible, we can look forward to a future where natural language processing plays an even greater role in our daily lives.

Collaborating with Chat GPT: Challenges and Benefits

A discussion of how businesses can work with the AI model

Chat GPT has revolutionized the way businesses operate and interact with their customers. From customer service to content creation, this powerful AI model has countless applications. However, businesses face challenges when working with such technology, and collaboration requires careful consideration and planning.

One of the primary challenges businesses face when working with Chat GPT is the need for domain-specific data. While the model has been trained on vast amounts of text data from the internet, it may not be optimized for specific industry jargon or niche topics. This means that businesses must provide the model with additional data to fine-tune it for their specific needs. Gathering and preparing this data can be a time-consuming and costly process.

Another challenge is the need for technical expertise to work with the model. While there are many tools and platforms available to simplify the process of training and deploying Chat GPT, businesses must still have individuals on their team who understand the technical details of working with AI models. This can be a significant investment for small businesses, and even larger organizations may struggle to find talent with the necessary expertise.

Despite these challenges, the benefits of working with Chat GPT can be substantial. One significant benefit is the ability to automate customer service through chatbots. By integrating Chat GPT into their chatbots, businesses can provide customers with fast and accurate responses to common questions, freeing up customer service representatives to handle more complex inquiries.

Chat GPT can also be used for content creation, helping businesses generate articles, social media posts, and other forms of content at scale. By automating the content creation process, businesses can save time and resources while still delivering high-quality content to their audience.

Additionally, Chat GPT can be used to gain insights into customer sentiment and preferences. By analyzing large amounts of text data, the model can identify patterns and trends in customer feedback, enabling businesses to make data-driven decisions.

While there are challenges to working with Chat GPT, the benefits can be substantial. By collaborating with this powerful AI model, businesses can automate processes, save time and resources, and gain valuable insights into customer behavior. With careful planning and a dedicated team, businesses can successfully integrate Chat GPT into their operations and gain a competitive advantage in their industry.

Exploring Chat GPT Competitors: Advantages and Disadvantages

In recent years, Chat GPT has emerged as a leading AI language model in the field of natural language processing. However, it is not the only AI language model available. There are other competitors in the market that are also vying for dominance. In this chapter, we will discuss the major competitors of Chat GPT, their advantages and disadvantages.

BERT (Bidirectional Encoder Representations from Transformers):

BERT, developed by Google, is a popular alternative to Chat GPT. One of the biggest advantages of BERT is that it is a bidirectional model, meaning it can take into account the context of words that appear both before and after a given word in a sentence. This allows BERT to better understand the meaning of complex sentences. However, one of the major drawbacks of BERT is that it requires a large amount of training data to achieve optimal performance.

XLNet:

XLNet is another transformer-based language model that was developed by researchers at Carnegie Mellon University and Google. XLNet has several advantages over Chat GPT, including the ability to model long-range dependencies between words and the ability to generate text in a more coherent and natural-sounding manner. However, one disadvantage of XLNet is that it is computationally expensive and requires a lot of processing power.

RoBERTa:

RoBERTa is a newer language model that was developed by Facebook. It is based on the BERT architecture but is trained on a larger amount of data and for a longer period of time. As a result, RoBERTa has achieved state-of-the-art performance on several natural language processing tasks. However, one disadvantage of RoBERTa is that it is not as interpretable as some other models, making it difficult to understand how it arrives at its predictions.

GShard:

GShard is a distributed training system developed by Google that can be used to train massive transformer-based language models, such as Chat GPT. One of the major advantages of GShard is that it allows for parallel training on multiple machines, which can significantly speed up the training process. However, one disadvantage of GShard is that it requires a lot of computing resources and is not as accessible to smaller organizations or individuals.

T5:

T5 is a transformer-based language model developed by Google that is trained on a wide range of tasks, including text generation, question answering, and translation. T5 has several advantages over Chat GPT, including the ability to handle a wider range of tasks and the ability to generate more coherent and natural-sounding text. However, one disadvantage of T5 is that it requires a large amount of training data and can be computationally expensive.

Chat GPT has several competitors in the field of natural language processing. Each model has its own advantages and disadvantages, and the choice of which model to use will depend on the specific task at hand and the available computing resources. However, Chat GPT remains a leading AI language model due to its versatility and ability to generate high-quality text.

The Endless Possibilities of Chat GPT

A look at the exciting potential of the technology

As we have seen throughout this book, Chat GPT represents a major breakthrough in natural language processing and has the potential to transform a wide range of industries. From customer service to content creation, Chat GPT's ability to generate human-like responses has already led to a range of exciting real-world applications.

But perhaps the most exciting thing about Chat GPT is that its potential uses are limited only by our imagination. As the technology continues to improve, we can expect to see even more innovative and impactful applications.

For businesses and organizations looking to incorporate Chat GPT into their operations, the benefits are clear. By using the AI model to handle repetitive or mundane tasks, employees can focus on more creative and high-level work. Additionally, Chat GPT can be used to improve customer service, enhance content creation, and automate various processes.

However, as with any emerging technology, there are also challenges to consider. Ethical concerns around AI and privacy are among the most pressing. It is important for businesses and organizations to be transparent about how they are using Chat GPT and to ensure that they are using the technology in an ethical manner.

Overall, Chat GPT represents a major step forward in the field of natural language processing, and its potential impact on society and business is truly exciting. As the technology continues to evolve, we can expect to see even more innovative applications and use cases emerge. By collaborating with Chat GPT, businesses and organizations can harness the power of this groundbreaking technology to drive innovation, improve operations, and deliver better experiences for customers and employees alike.

....

END.

www.ingramcontent.com/pod-product-compliance
Lightning Source LLC
LaVergne TN
LVHW051615050326
832903LV00033B/4517